The Royal Engagement   *24th February 1981*

The Wedding
St Paul's Cathedral   *29th July 1981*

Acknowledgments
   The photographs in this book appear by courtesy of the following:
BBC, pages 15 (bottom), 28, 30; Camera Press, pages 4, 8, 13, 35 (top),
37 (top right); Daily Telegraph, pages 36, 37; *Diver* magazine, page 46;
Fox Photos, pages 7, 10 (top), 14, 15 (top), 17, 34, 40 (top), 49; Anwar
Hussein, cover and pages 20, 21, 22, 23, 25, 26, 27, 31 (top), 35
(bottom), 39, 40 (bottom), 42 (bottom), 43, 45 (middle), 46, 47, 50, 51;
Keystone Press, pages 6, 10 (bottom), 11, 12; Serge Lemoine, page 38;
Paul Popper Ltd, pages 9, 24, 44 (right); Press Association Ltd, page 44
(centre), and back cover; John Scott, pages 5, 16, 18, 19, 29, 31, 32, 33,
41, 42 (top), 45.
   The family tree on the back endpaper was prepared by Mr R M Powell.
   Designed by Ian Thewlis, reproduction by Victor Ward of Leicester.

First edition 23rd March 1981

© LADYBIRD BOOKS LTD MCMLXXXI

HRH Prince Charles

written by IAN A MORRISON MA PhD

Ladybird Books Loughborough

At quarter past nine on the evening of 14th November 1948, a baby was born in Buckingham Palace. Soon a policeman at the gates shouted to the waiting crowd that they had a prince. At midnight they were still cheering so lustily that the policemen asked for a bit of quiet for those in the Palace, but the crowd were still there at 2 o'clock in the morning.

Although some are against the whole idea of Royalty, in Britain a great many people like having a Royal family to represent the nation — a family which does not claim political power, or owe its position to party politics like the presidents of many other countries. The Royal family offers a more permanent symbol for the nation, for its family history is woven through the history of Britain.

The new prince, Charles, is descended not only. from James (VI of Scotland and I of England) who united the crowns of Great Britain, but from Llewelyn, Prince of All Wales, and on the Irish side from the High Kings of Erin. He is related through his father, Prince Philip Duke of Edinburgh, to Harold II, the last Anglo-Saxon King, and through his mother to William the Conqueror.

When Charles was scarcely three years old, his well-loved grandfather, King George VI, died, and his mother, Princess Elizabeth, became Queen Elizabeth II. This made him heir to the throne, which means that he should in turn become King after her reign.

How should a prince be brought up in the last half of the 20th century? It was decided he should go to school. This was a bolder step than it perhaps seems. No heir before him had ever done this. They had been taught by tutors in the privacy of the palaces.

By going out to school, that privacy was lost.
Growing up can be quite difficult enough at times
even if you have not been born a prince or princess,
but if you *have* been, anything you do (or don't do!)
may be reported and flashed round the world as a
news story, for thousands of people to see, whether
you like it or not.

Reporters and photographers can be very
determined. The boarding schools to which Prince
Charles went gave a chance of more privacy than a
state school, but it still must have been very difficult
for him. He seems to have found it hard to find real
friends among the boys. Some might pretend to
befriend him so that they could boast about knowing
a prince, others would avoid him altogether so that
they could not be accused of being snobbish.

As he drew towards the end of his school-days, things took a turn for the better. Because the Royal Family has a worldwide role in the Commonwealth, it seemed a good idea for Prince Charles to go to Australia on a school exchange.

He went to Timbertop, part of Geelong Grammar School. Unlike the main school, it is about a hundred and sixty kilometres away from Melbourne, set among gum trees in a huge outback estate. There in the bush he was far from the advice of his family, but he was now seventeen, and also free of many of the pressures on him in Britain. As the Headmaster pointed out, before his visit most Australians knew little if anything about Prince Charles.

This was no disadvantage. Looking back, Prince Charles has said that Australia helped him over his shyness. When he was on a trip to New Guinea, his plane landed at Brisbane to refuel, and he was confronted by what he described as a terrifying sea of faces. But as he walked towards them, he says something 'clicked' inside him, and he has never since felt nervous in public (though this was something that had troubled his grandfather, George VI, throughout his reign).

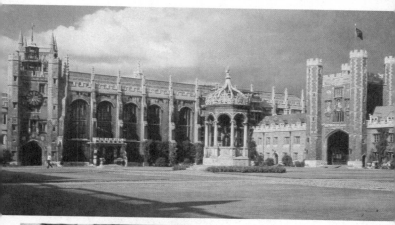

Prince Charles had of course been too small to take part in shaping the decision that made him the first heir to the throne to go out to school. However, he was now old enough to share in the decision on the next step. He was keen to go to university to follow up his interest in history and archaeology, and in October 1967 he set off for Trinity College, Cambridge.

This time it was not a sea of faces that confronted him but of legs. As he explained later in a student

magazine, he knew he was to be met by the Master and Senior Tutor, but when he arrived, wedged into a Mini, the crowd closed in and all he could see were "serried ranks of variously trousered legs" — from which he had to try to pick out the right pairs. Despite this beginning, and all the inevitable disruptions of his studies by his royal duties, in 1970 he graduated with an honours B.A. degree. He also enjoyed himself.

He enjoyed his archaeology and history, but he also had fun of a lighter kind with student theatre shows. When he had been at school in Scotland he had shown talent for serious acting in Shakespeare's *Macbeth*, but he had also played the Pirate King there in *The Pirates of Penzance*, and he had long been a fan of The Goons, Morecambe and Wise, and Tommy Cooper.

At Cambridge he joined in all kinds of revue sketches, including one inspired by the dustman who used to wake him up by singing under his window while emptying bins early in the morning.

above: *On stage in a Cambridge revue*
opposite: *Charles as* Macbeth *at Gordonstoun School*

He made music of his own too. When he was
younger, he tried the piano and then the trumpet,
but after hearing Jacqueline du Pré play at the
London Festival Hall his imagination was caught by
the rich tones of the cello, and he took it up while
still at school. He continued with it at university,
and played in the college orchestra.

It is not only through theatre and music that he
has a practical interest in the arts. His first ever
school report said, "Art: good and simply loves
drawing and painting," and he has kept that up
when he has had time, too.

However pleasant, these kinds of activities can only be fitted in to whatever time is left over from the main art that he must study: the art of being a Prince, and in time a King.

When he was finishing university, like all students he was given a booklet on *Choosing a Career*, but there has been little choice for him, from the time he was born.

Knowing what lay ahead of him, the Queen and Prince Philip at first gave him as near to a normal childhood as could be managed, letting him grow up gradually into realising that he was 'not just an ordinary chap', but somebody people were interested in, with special duties and responsibilities.

In his early years, many requests for the little prince to make public appearances were turned down, but then he was introduced to a regular part in Royal Family events, before emerging through Timbertop as a public figure in his own right. By the time he was at university he was making his own public speeches and handling his first radio, TV and newspaper interviews for himself.

In learning how to cope with state duties, his mother the Queen must always have been a leading influence on him, but his father has clearly also played a major part in shaping his style. Indeed, when Prince Charles was little, some people thought that he just mimicked his father's mannerisms. But that is a stage many small boys pass through, and as he grew up writers often commented on contrasts in personality and interests between father and son. There are of course family resemblances: their lively style on walkabouts, the way they laugh (and what they laugh about!) and so on.

The father taught his son to swim, and to shoot, fish and sail, and introduced him to the excitements of polo, a ball game played from horseback which they clearly both enjoy.

Otherwise, Charles has never been as interested in team games as his father, but seems to have a taste for more solitary pastimes and to be more involved with the arts and particularly his music. His father sometimes looks less than happy when he has to sit through a long concert!

One serious activity that the prince shares with his
parents is the encouragement of British industry.
They clearly feel that since they belong to an
industrialised country of the 20th century, this is as
much part of their job as is the pageantry of the
great state occasions that remind people of the
historical roots that bind the nation together. Now
he is often invited to try ou ultra-modern machines,
like the moon buggy.

The Queen's Awards for Export are an example of one type of royal encouragement; Prince Philip is known for another kind. Although he is the Queen's husband he is not a king, so he can speak out more freely as an individual than she can as Monarch. He has developed a reputation for encouraging more effort by making witty but hardhitting speeches, suggesting that things might be done better in Britain by managers and work people alike. Prince Charles has joined in this, and his speeches too are anything but pompous. He says that he believes humour is a very useful way of getting people to listen to what you are saying. The practice in acting he enjoyed at school and university has helped him to develop the sense of timing (and of the ridiculous) that makes him an effective public speaker.

Driving the astronauts' moon buggy

It is by no means only within the British Isles that the Royal Family play their 20th century parts. They act as very special ambassadors, able to stand outside party politics in making their good-will visits to countries all over the world. In particular they serve as a symbolic link for the scattered countries of the Commonwealth, helping to keep them together as a family of nations in a difficult world. In achieving this, the Queen has travelled more than any previous monarch in British history.

A visit to the Budhanilkantha school in Nepal

Charles was just five when he was taken on his first long trip, to Malta to meet his parents on their way home from the coronation tour of the Commonwealth. Since then, the mileage has built up for him too. For example, when he was finishing

Wearing African robes in Ghana

university in 1970 he had to sandwich the work for his degree (and for his pilot's licence) into a year that started with a trip to Strasbourg for a Conservation Conference and ended with President de Gaulle's funeral in Paris. In between, he had been round the world three times, to visit the people of Australia, New Zealand, Japan, Canada, the United States, Bermuda, Barbados and various Pacific islands.

In the Arctic Circle

What do you say to a man whose job is collecting poison from snakes?

As he moves into the 1980s, Prince Charles has thus a great deal of experience behind him as representative of his country.

Not only the thousands of kilometres of fast travel but the necessity of being unfailingly polite, however tired you may be, and of showing an interest in hundreds of people you don't know, must be a great strain. As he has remarked wryly, if it were not for his ability to see the funny side of his life, he might have been "committed to an institution" long ago. But the humour that comes across in his speeches obviously stands him in good stead, helping him to relax tension not only for other people but for

himself as well. It's said for instance that when he turned up for a formal event in Edinburgh in a

simple dinner jacket, to find everyone else resplendent in full evening dress with tail coats, he asked them why they had all dressed up as butlers . . .

And when he hurried back after three weeks living rough with Royal Marine Commandos in the Canadian bush, he enjoyed the appropriateness of being made Great Master of the Order of the Bath by his mother . . .

Sport offers him one way of relaxing. He is best at polo but has had a go at many things (he has even been seen on a skateboard!) But if you are a prince, it is very difficult to pursue your hobbies without being pursued yourself. Even when he has gone stalking a stag in remote Scottish glens, he has found himself being stalked in turn by photographers with telephoto lenses.

Sometimes, faced by the never-ending pursuit of the pressmen when he has wanted to relax, he has managed to turn this into a kind of sport in its own right. He has become an expert and adventurous skier, and has had fun leading the reporters on wild chases down mountains in Canada and Switzerland. It is said that some journalists have taken special skiing lessons to try to keep up with him!

Press photographers wait for a Royal appearance

Trotting in Scotland

Like most members of the Royal Family, Prince Charles is keen on horses. Besides being a polo player of international standard, he rides to hounds, goes in for cross-country team riding, and has been seen on the racecourse as an amateur jockey.

Again, every move is followed by the press. He has explained that when you are doing something competitive like that in public, it is easy to feel it is only when you fall off that reporters are interested and that photographs only appear when you are upside down or halfway up a tree . . .

Occasionally cameramen get in the way, sometimes not entirely by accident. For example, when he was wind-surfing, the wake from a camera-boat kept overturning him, giving excellent pictures of him falling in . . .

The continual pressure and lack of privacy must be wearing, but the prince has had to come to terms with it as he has grown up. As he has put it, in his kind of job, there would not be much point in being around if nobody wanted to write about you or photograph you.

Against all these pressures, it seems clear that the strength of the Royal Family lies in the fact that it *is* a family, and rather a happy one. Prince Charles has often said he is happier at home than anywhere else.

In his position it is very difficult to find people outside the family to whom you can talk really freely, and with whom you can be confident of the kind of personal privacy in which most other people can expect to live their lives. As his father once put it, royal children soon find it is much safer to unburden themselves to a member of the family than to a friend, because even a small indiscretion can lead to all sorts of difficulties.

His mother had her own happy childhood to model theirs upon, and they have grown up as a close-knit group, each encouraged to develop his or

her own individuality, confident in the basic unity of the family. Prince Philip has let it be known that decisions have often been discussed by family 'committee'.

Even when he is far overseas, Charles is often in touch with them by letter or telephone.

All the Family

The royal children fall into two groups by age. Princess Anne is less than two years younger than Charles, and is now married to Captain Mark Phillips, with a family of her own. As a child she was reckoned to be the more boisterous character. It is said that she found, to her delight, that enormous guardsmen in their bearskins crashed to attention and presented arms to even the tiniest of princesses, and that she made a game of this that kept the Palace sentries busy . . .

Prince Andrew and Prince Edward are 12 and 16 years younger than Charles respectively. When they were little, Prince Charles wrote them a story about an Old Man who lived in a cave at Lochnagar in Scotland once upon a time, when knees were especially hairy. He was carried off by an eagle, and dropped from a great height onto a trampoline the royal children had at Balmoral, their home in the Highlands.

Now Andrew as well as Charles has grown up to do his own parachuting. While Edward still has a little while to go as a "little brother", Andrew has more than caught up with Charles in height.

When Prince Charles himself was small, one person who was especially kind to him was his grandmother, Queen Elizabeth the Queen Mother. They have remained good friends ever since, and it is pleasant to see, through thirty years of news films, first the grandmother looking after the little boy and then the fully grown prince escorting his grandmother in his turn. There is clearly a particular affection between them, and it is said that her wiseness

helped him through some of the difficult patches in growing up.

They obviously enjoy lighter moments together too. From her childhood in the north of Scotland onwards, the Queen Mother has been a keen angler, and when he was little she taught him fly-fishing. Ever since then they have enjoyed going fishing together, and not only in British rivers. When he was at Timbertop, she visited Australia, and they went off to live in a cabin and try their hands at fishing the streams of the Snowy Mountains. We don't know what she had to say about his Timbertop tale of rustling kangaroos by creeping up on them from behind and grabbing them by the tail to flick them over on their backs . . .

It was in the streams at Balmoral that the Queen Mother had taught Charles to fish. He has always enjoyed holidays there.

At first he was not nearly as happy with his other main contact with Scotland, Gordonstoun, where he spent the last four years of his schooldays. Although his father, Prince Philip, had been at school there, tales Prince Charles heard before he got there made the rigorous boarding school sound 'pretty gruesome'. Its aim was to inspire boys to stretch their physical and mental capacities to their limits, and in many ways it did prove very hard going, especially because

of the extra pressures on him as a prince (some of his class essays even disappeared, to be published without permission in foreign magazines). Nevertheless, by the end he decided he was glad he had gone there. He said that Gordonstoun had indeed developed his will power, self control and self discipline.

His official connections with Scotland include titles and offices that range from Colonel-in-Chief of the Gordon Highlanders through Duke of Rothesay, Earl of Carrick and Baron Renfrew, to Lord of the Isles and Great Steward of Scotland.

All being well, Prince Charles will succeed to the crowns of Scotland and England in due course. He is already Prince of Wales.

He was nine when the Queen announced this, saying to the Welsh people that she would present him to them at Caernarvon Castle when he was grown up. This is what is called the 'investiture' of the Prince, and before him only the Duke of Windsor had been invested there.

Although since mediaeval times there had been twenty earlier English Princes of Wales, many of whom had become Kings of England, few had identified themselves much with Welsh culture or interests. Charles is the first to be descended directly from both the great native Welsh princely lines of Owen Glendower and Llewelyn-ap-Gruffydd, but some modern Welsh Nationalists still regarded him as an unacceptable foreigner, and threats were even

made against his life. However, he showed his willingness to support his involvement with Wales by hard work, firstly by studying the language and the culture of the country intensively at University in Aberystwyth. By the time of his investiture in 1969, an opinion poll showed that 90% of the Welsh were in favour of the ceremony, and since then he has shown a continuing commitment to Welsh affairs, from countryside conservation and industry, to music and rugby.

His investiture as Prince of Wales was just one of the extraordinary variety of ceremonies in which he has to play a leading part, both at home and abroad. These range from state weddings and funerals and openings of parliaments, through military, civil and religious events of every kind, indoors and outdoors.

On duty in Fiji

The mediaeval ritual for the investiture of a Knight of the Garter in Windsor Castle is of course quite different from the kind of modern pageantry of Independence Celebrations in the Bahamas or Fiji. But every eye and camera is on the prince, and the world just assumes that he will get his timing right, remember which way to turn, and not drop his sword. *He* can assume nothing however. Every detail has to be prepared and memorised, and it is lucky that he has a talent and liking for both history and acting.

Yet to be good at the ceremonial side is not enough. To succeed with the modern task of the

British royalty, symbolising not only the nation's heritage but seeking to strengthen bridges between people, it is not enough to be a detached ceremonial figure. Prince Charles aims to be just as good at chatting with people in factory canteens as at making speeches at formal banquets. As he has himself said, the whole idea of these visits is for him to meet as many people as he can, so that they can see for themselves that he's what he calls a pretty ordinary sort of person.

At many of the ceremonies that he attends, Prince Charles appears in the uniform of one or another of the Queen's services. Very often, to match the pageantry of the events, these are full-dress uniforms resplendent with rich colours, ornamental sashes and lanyards, heraldic badges and magnificent headgear.

With his parachute badge on his shoulder

However, he is by no means only a ceremonial soldier, sailor or airman. In a tradition that goes back to the young knights of mediaeval times *earning* their spurs, he has trained with each of the Services whose uniform he wears.

Thus the little badge showing a parachute with wings that you may notice on his uniform at the Trooping of the Colour for the Queen's Birthday is not just an ornament. It means that he went through tough paratroop training with the Commandos, becoming the first Prince of Wales in history to make parachute jumps.

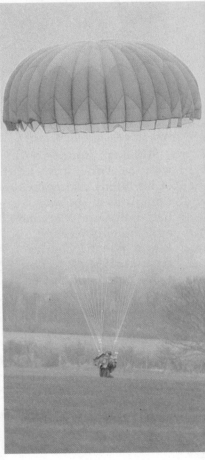

On the first one, he was whipped upside down and his feet caught in the parachute lines. He untangled himself quite safely on the way down to the sea below (though he doesn't tell us if the jerk made him swallow the Polo mint Flight Sergeant Kidd had given him in the aircraft just before he jumped!)

With Lord Louis Mountbatten

Although Prince Charles has his lively contacts with the Army, it is with the Navy that the traditions of his family are most closely associated. Prince Philip was in the sea battle off Cape Matapan as a young officer in World War II. Charles' great-uncle the late Lord Louis Mountbatten (a particular friend to him in both boyhood and manhood) had commanded *HMS Kelly* in the thick of fighting, and Charles' grandfather and great-grandfather had both had naval careers before becoming Kings George VI and V.

Prince Charles first went to the Royal Naval College at Dartmouth, and then over the next five years served on ships large and small until in 1976 he was appointed commander of *HMS Bronington*, a little mine-sweeper called after a Welsh village. On top of carrying out all the normal duties of a naval officer, the prince had to keep up with his royal duties, studying state papers, preparing for royal functions and coping with sacks of correspondence each week. Yet it is clear that he enjoyed life at sea, where for once he could get to know small groups of people of varied backgrounds, well away from the pressures of publicity. Through his responsibility for his men's welfare, he could get insights into the problems of others. As one of his captains put it, where else could a future king learn how difficult it is to keep a wife and family together during long separations, and on a limited budget?

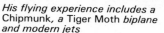

His flying experience includes a
Chipmunk, *a* Tiger Moth *biplane*
and modern jets

While in the Navy, Prince Charles qualified as an
operational helicopter combat pilot. That is not an
easy thing to do, but he has always been keen on
flying and first went 'solo' in a little Chipmunk
trainer when he was twenty. Three years later he
joined the Royal Air Force, having to try to complete
a twelve month course in five months because of
time pressure from his royal duties. Besides learning
to handle jets in the air, this meant he had to study
subjects such as aerodynamics, meteorology and

navigation. These all involved mathematics, which he had always found something of a misery. Yet he had to pass, and he did.

His report said that in the air he showed a natural aptitude at flying, was good at aerobatics and would make an excellent pilot of supersonic fighters.

Since then he has flown many kinds of aircraft, from a World War II Spitfire to an enormous Vulcan, and like Prince Philip, who is also a keen pilot, he is often to be seen at the controls of aircraft of the Queen's Flight, keeping his hand in by flying himself to and from his royal visits.

Prince Charles goes down as well as up. Part of his naval training before going on submarine patrol included a practice underwater escape from 30 metres down, without breathing apparatus. He has also trained to use aqualungs as a frogman, and has even dived under the ice nearly 800 kilometres north of the Arctic Circle. Besides seeing the work that a Canadian scientist was doing there, he had a go at walking about upside down in the roof of pack ice, watching his bubbles spread out like pools of shimmering mercury on the underside of the ice.

Some of the most interesting royal dives have been nearer home however, when he has visited the archaeologists working underwater on the wreck of the *Mary Rose*. She sank in the Solent off Portsmouth in the south of England when Henry VIII's navy was fighting off a French attack in 1545. All kinds of things have been preserved intact in the mud there. Not only Tudor cannons on their wooden gun carriages but everything from longbows to the surgeon's ointment pots. There is even a *shawm*: a kind of oboe. Henry VIII himself may have heard it played when he dined aboard *Mary Rose* shortly before she was lost. He too was a man of action with a liking for music, like his royal descendant Prince Charles.

Ready to dive to the Mary Rose

Finding a suitable wife is difficult enough at the best of times, and finding one who can also take on all the problems of becoming a Queen one day must be doubly hard. Deciding whether you have met the right partner is one of the most personal and private things in most people's lives, so imagine what it is like when the public all over the world is interested in you, and press men follow your every move trying to get 'the news' before their rivals. Rumours spread with the slightest excuse.

With pressures like this upon him, it is perhaps hardly surprising that the Prince avoided haste in his decision, and he was thirty two years old when the Palace announced his engagement to Lady Diana Spencer on February 24th, 1981.

He had been described as 'the most eligible bachelor in the world', so it is rather pleasant that in the tradition of the best fairy tales, the prince chose to marry 'the girl next door'. Lady Diana was born at Park House, Sandringham, next to the royal family's country home there. She was no stranger to the problems of royal life, because her father was the Queen's Equerry, and her grandmother is a Lady-in-waiting to the Queen Mother. Her bearing while under considerable pressure from the press revealed her innate ability to handle difficult situations under stress.

She is the daughter of Edward, 8th Earl Spencer, and she and Prince Charles share a common ancestor in James VI of Scotland (James I of Great Britain).

They share common interests too. They are fond of outdoor pursuits — both enjoy ski-ing, and are keen swimmers — and both love music.

Prince Charles has been heard to call himself a jack-of-all-trades. Certainly it seems that a prince in his time wears many hats.

He has worn some that no other Prince of Wales before him has worn, and done things that no other

has done, such as being not only the first to earn a university degree but even the first to go to school.

Some of the things he has done have been spectacular, like being the first to parachute, dive or learn to fly (indeed he went on to join the Ten Ton Club by piloting an aircraft at over 1000 miles per hour). One critic of royalty has claimed he behaves like this just to fill in his time, and others have dismissed him as just a 'Court Jester'. But in the complicated and often tense world of the present day there is little place for a distant humourless and boring figurehead. He has said he sees his basic aims as showing concern for people, displaying interest in them as individuals, and encouraging them in a whole host of ways.

Surely a prince who is not only interested in his people but who is himself an interesting and humorous individual has a better prospect of succeeding in the royal role at this end of the 20th century?

The lines of descent

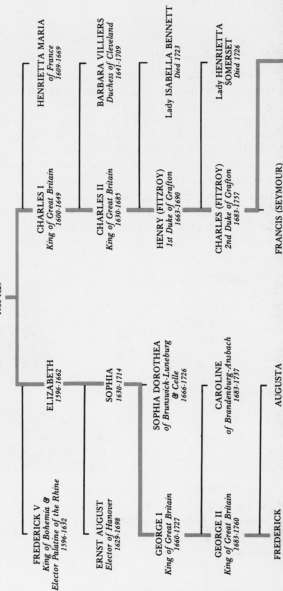

JAMES VI and I
King of Great Britain
1566-1625

FREDERICK V
King of Bohemia &
Elector Palatine of the Rhine
1596-1632

ELIZABETH
1596-1662

CHARLES I
King of Great Britain
1600-1649

HENRIETTA MARIA
of France
1609-1669

ERNST AUGUST
Elector of Hanover
1629-1698

SOPHIA
1630-1714

CHARLES II
King of Great Britain
1630-1685

BARBARA VILLIERS
Duchess of Cleveland
1641-1709

GEORGE I
King of Great Britain
1660-1727

SOPHIA DOROTHEA
of Brunswick-Luneburg
& Celle
1666-1726

HENRY (FITZROY)
1st Duke of Grafton
1663-1690

Lady ISABELLA BENNETT
Died 1723

GEORGE II
King of Great Britain
1683-1760

CAROLINE
of Brandenburg-Ansbach
1683-1737

CHARLES (FITZROY)
2nd Duke of Grafton
1683-1757

Lady HENRIETTA
SOMERSET
Died 1726

FREDERICK

AUGUSTA

FRANCIS (SEYMOUR)